# PERGAMON INTERNATIONAL LIBRARY
## of Science, Technology, Engineering and Social Studies

*The 1000-volume original paperback library in aid of education,
industrial training and the enjoyment of leisure*

Publisher: Rob~~ert Maxwell, M.C.~~

## Other Titles of Interest

DAVIS, S. M.
Managing and Organizing Multinational Corporations

HORI, T.
·The Japanese and the Australians: Business and Cultural Exchange

KILMARX, R. & ALEXANDER, Y.
Business and the Middle East: Threats and Prospects

McARA, P.
Marketing to Australian Industry

THORELLI, H. B. & BECKER, H.
International Marketing Strategy, rev. ed.

SASAKI, N.
Management and Industrial Structure in Japan

## Related Journal

OMEGA*

The International Journal of Management Science
*Chief Editor:* Samuel Eilon, Imperial College of Science and Technology,
London, UK.

OMEGA provides all specialists in management science with important new
developments in operational research and managerial economics. Published
material ranges from original contributions to review articles describing the
state-of-the-art in specific areas, together with shorter critical assessment of
particular management techniques.

*Free specimen copy available on request.

# Exporting to the UK

## A BASIC GUIDE FOR THE DEVELOPING COUNTRY EXPORTER

*Prepared by the United Kingdom Trade Agency for Developing Countries utilising various source materials*

*Compiled and edited by*

*RODNEY ALLEN*

## PERGAMON PRESS

OXFORD · NEW YORK · TORONTO · SYDNEY · PARIS · FRANKFURT

| U.K. | Pergamon Press Ltd., Headington Hill Hall, Oxford OX3 0BW, England |
|------|------|
| U.S.A. | Pergamon Press Inc., Maxwell House, Fairview Park, Elmsford, New York 10523, U.S.A. |
| CANADA | Pergamon Press Canada Ltd., Suite 104, 150 Consumers Rd., Willowdale, Ontario M2J 1P9, Canada |
| AUSTRALIA | Pergamon Press (Aust.) Pty. Ltd., P.O. Box 544, Potts Point, N.S.W. 2011, Australia |
| FRANCE | Pergamon Press SARL, 24 rue des Ecoles, 75240 Paris, Cedex 05, France |
| FEDERAL REPUBLIC OF GERMANY | Pergamon Press GmbH, Hammerweg 6, D-6242 Kronberg-Taunus, Federal Republic of Germany |

First edition 1983

**Library of Congress Cataloging in Publication Data**

Main entry under title:
Exporting to the UK.
(Pergamon international library of science, technology, engineering, and social studies)
Includes index.
1. Great Britain—Commerce—Handbooks, manuals, etc.
I. United Kingdom Trade Agency for Developing Countries.
II. Series.
HF3507.E95   1983       658.8'48'0941       82-24691

**British Library Cataloguing in Publication Data**

Exporting to the UK.—(Pergamon international library)
1. Underdeveloped areas—Commerce—Great Britain.
2. Great Britain—Commerce—Underdeveloped areas.
I. Title    II. United Kingdom
Trade Agency.
382'6'01724       HF1413

ISBN 0-08-030205-X

*Printed in Great Britain by A. Wheaton & Co. Ltd. Exeter*

# Contents

# Exporting to Britain

Over the centuries Britain has established a tradition of open trade in which
the new trader should generally find himself welcome. Moreover, the range
of goods imported is extremely varied and there are few goods for which
there are no importers interested in learning of a new source of supply.
Providing an exporter selling to the UK is prepared to persevere and
ensure that his goods reach the quality required, and that his prices are
competitive, then, hopefully, he should succeed in the long run.

Of course, it would be wrong to ignore the problems facing the developing-country exporter whose experience may be confined to supplying a
highly-protected home market, or to meeting local tastes which have little
counterpart in the UK. In such cases, the exporter's goods may require
substantial modification. Nevertheless, if the potential exporter takes the
trouble to study carefully what is being sold in the UK market, keeps in
continual touch with his UK business contacts and is prepared where necessary to invest in new plant, he should be able to overcome these problems.
However, this publication assumes that the developing-country businessman
already has suitable goods for export but is concerned about the basic
skills and knowledge required when exporting. The following pages should
assist him by supplying background information on the UK, comments on
export terminology and a step-by-step analysis of export transactions in
general.

## British Overseas Trade and Imports

UK trade in goods and services represents over 30% of the gross domestic
product at factor cost. This is a higher proportion than any other industrialised economy of equivalent size. In 1980 visible imports amounted to
around £50,000 million, of which some 12% was accounted for by food,
beverages and tobacco, some 8% by basic raw materials and the remainder
by semi-processed and finished manufactures (see Appendix B for a

breakdown of trade figures). Of this total expenditure on visible imports, £5686 million (11.4%) came from non-oil exporting developing countries.

*UK Consumer Expenditure*

Consumer expenditure *per capita* in 1980 was £2419. This was divided as follows:

| | | |
|---|---|---|
| Food (household expenditure) | £411 | (17%) |
| Alcoholic drink | £194 | (8%) |
| Tobacco | £97 | (4%) |
| Housing (including mortgage payments) | £363 | (15%) |
| Fuel and light | £121 | (5%) |
| Clothing and footwear | £161 | (7%) |
| Durable goods | £218 | (9%) |
| Running cost of motor vehicles | £145 | (6%) |
| Travel | £73 | (3%) |
| Meals and accommodation outside th  ome | £120 | (5%) |
| Other goods | £266 | (11%) |
| Services | £242 | (10%) |

In 1979, 57.9% of households had cars, 55% some form of central heating, 76.6% washing machines, 92.9% refrigerators, 95.8% TV sets, 67.2% telephones.

*Population and Distribution*

The current UK population is about 56 million. The UK ranks fourteenth in the world in population size. About half the population lives in a belt stretching from Yorkshire and Lancashire in North Central England to Greater London in the south-east. Greater London is the most concentrated population area with some 6.7 million people; other important population areas are Central Clydeside in Scotland, Greater Manchester, Merseyside, South Yorkshire, Tyne and Wear, West Midlands and West Yorkshire. Average population density is 229 per sq. km. However, certain parts of the United Kingdom, like Central Wales and Northern Scotland, are sparsely populated.

## Import Channels

The UK trading/distribution system generally offers a wide range of choices for the exporter wishing to sell his goods in the British market. The approach he adopts will depend to a large extent upon his product. In timber, for instance, he might sell through a commission agent with the actual importing done by a timber merchant or timber-using firm. In canned goods or clothing, he might sell direct to major retail groups or, alternatively, through an importer/wholesaler or distributor. On the whole, the UK internal trading system is efficient and goods reach the retail trade stage with relatively modest mark-ups. However, margins, particularly at the retail stage, will tend to be higher on non-essential, non-branded goods whose stock turnover is relatively slow. In some cases, the difference between CIF price and the retail price can be considerable.

The exporter's goods may pass through a number of hands before they reach the final consumer. However, the exporter will be concerned primarily with his business point of entry into the UK market. Such an entry point, depending upon the circumstances, may be one of the following:

(a) Commission agent who acts for the exporter in exchange for a commission and does not buy for his own account. Importation may be organised by the exporter himself or by the agent on behalf of his customers in the UK.

(b) Importer trader who buys for his own account and organises importation, but sells on the goods promptly, often before they arrive in the UK.

(c) Importer merchant who imports the goods and holds them in order to supply customers on demand from his warehouse.

(d) Importer wholesaler is similar to the merchant except that there will be a greater emphasis on selling and distribution in the UK market. The wholesaler is likely to have a sales force, delivery vehicles, etc.

(e) Distributor agent who acts on the exporter's behalf, often in exchange for an agreed price discount, and holds the goods in his warehouse and arranges for their effective distribution in the UK.

(f) Importer retailer who imports the goods in order to sell on direct to the individual customer. Due to the growth of large retail chains, this type of importer is becoming increasingly important in foodstuffs and household consumer goods.

(g) Importer manufacturer who imports raw materials or semi-processed goods, directly for his own use, rather than utilising the services of an importer trader or importer merchant.

(h) Finally, the exporter should not ignore the importance of UK-based export houses who import goods into the UK for immediate re-export to customers abroad, or who themselves often ship direct from the supplier's (exporter's) country to non-UK customers.

## The Distribution System

There were 2.8 million employees in the distributive trade in mid-1979, of which about three-fifths were retailing and the remainder in trading and wholesaling. There are some 350,000 retail outlets in the UK, of which 130,000 are concerned with grocery and other food products, nearly 60,000 with tobacco and confectionery, some 60,000 with clothing, footwear, etc., approximately the same number concerned with other household consumer goods and some 65,000 in other products. Mail-order distribution should not be neglected. About 16 million shop regularly by post through catalogues.

One of the most significant trends in recent years has been the increase in the proportion of retail turnover handled by large multiple groups. In the grocery trade, Sainsbury, Tesco, Asda, Fine Fare, Kwiksave and International Stores are some leading companies worthy of note. In general consumer goods, including textiles, Marks and Spencer, British Home Stores, Debenhams, House of Fraser and Woolworths might be mentioned; in chemist goods, Boots; in photographic and electronic products, Dixons; and in books, games and stationery, W. H. Smith. Some of the larger groups have sales approaching £2000 million per annum.

A number of the large retail groups may also undertake some wholesaling, that is selling to stores outside their own organisation. Numerous specialised wholesalers exist in most product groups, such as Booker McConnell and Linfood in grocery products. New Covent Garden — which is an association of wholesalers — plays a leading role in the distribution of fruit and vegetables.

## Market Requirements

Due to the enormous range of articles available in the UK market, it is difficult to generalise. Quality of goods will be more important in some cases than others. Certain goods, such as foodstuffs and electrical equipment, will have to meet minimum standards or they cannot be imported. In other cases, quality may be sacrificed up to a point providing the price is sufficiently attractive. However, presentation, packaging, and design will always be important. A product has not only to be sound, but also visually acceptable.

*Agencies*

There is at present no specialised law regarding the appointment and rights of agents in the UK. The exporter is free to appoint agents on an exclusive or non-exclusive basis, or not at all. When appointing an agent, the exporter must consider carefully the typical distribution and marketing factors related to his goods. If the exporter's goods are of a type which is normally heavily promoted in the UK market, then it may be desirable to appoint an exclusive agency to provide the incentive for undertaking such promotional activities. An agent should have the resources as well as the interest to promote actively the exporter's goods. It may be important that he has facilities for wholesaling and distribution. If the agent has exclusive representation for the import of the goods into the UK, then the exporter should obtain the agent's firm commitment to find a market for a satisfactory quantity of the goods during an agreed time period. If he fails to meet that target, he will not be reappointed.

*Import Assistance*

The exporter can contact the United Kingdom Trade Agency for Developing Countries (UKTA), which is an import promotion office established by the British Government to assist exporters from developing countries as part of the UK Aid Programme. This organisation will suggest suitable trade contacts and provide other helpful information of assistance to exporters. Such assistance is given without charge.

The Tropical Products Institute (TPI) is another Government organisation able to answer enquiries specifically related to agricultural products. It can advise on quality and marketability and publishes an extensive range of product market studies.

The British Importers Confederation (BIC) is an organisation representing a number of trade associations and individual members engaged in importing into the UK. Membership is about 3500 and is open to foreign companies engaged in exporting to the UK through its International Membership Division. The BIC publishes the *Directory of British Importers* and the *Directory of British Clothing and Textile Importers*. It circulates regularly, free of charge, notices by overseas exporters seeking importers and trading partners in the UK.

Chambers of Commerce in the UK can also be approached by overseas exporters and will circulate their members with details of goods which may be of interest to importers amongst their membership. The London Chamber of Commerce and Industry is the largest UK Chamber and issues a regular bulletin of trade opportunities entitled "Openings for Trade".

See Appendix D for addresses.

# Outline Export Activities Flow Chart

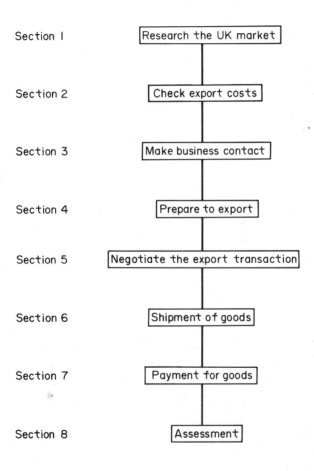

Section 1      Research the UK market

Section 2      Check export costs

Section 3      Make business contact

Section 4      Prepare to export

Section 5      Negotiate the export transaction

Section 6      Shipment of goods

Section 7      Payment for goods

Section 8      Assessment

# Export Activities Checklist

INTRODUCTION

In exporting, the number and range of activities in which the exporter is involved are substantial, complex and highly technical. The checklist of activities itemised in the following pages is not presumed to be exhaustive as most export transactions will have special features that would require a much larger publication than this to cover adequately. Thus, it is intended only to cover typical features in exporting from the point of view of an inexperienced exporter. Nor is it possible in the space available to deal in detail with the very many technical aspects of shipping goods, such as documentation and obtaining payments, which the exporter will have to face. The object of this publication is to treat these subjects in broad outline with a view to providing some guidance in approaching more specialist publications, and also to assist the exporter in his discussions with forwarding agents and banks, who will almost certainly be involved in one way or another in every export transaction.

The list of activities has been divided into eight main sections. A checklist is given for each section together with comments on each element of the checklist. Although the flow chart of activities and the order of the sections are presented as a simple straight sequence, many activities under one section will be related to activities listed in another section. This is particularly so in Sections 6 and 7, which concern the shipment of goods and payment for them. When important, reference to such a relationship is mentioned in the text. Nevertheless, the broad order of activities is valid as set forth.

A brief comment is required on Section 4 — Prepare to Export. This stage should not be confused with the activities outlined in Section 6 — Shipment of Goods. Before he attempts to negotiate an export transaction, the exporter must have acquired as far as possible all the information he needs as a result of activities listed in the first three sections. If, due to an obvious lack of knowledge or foresight, he finds himself unprepared when he undertakes serious export negotiations, he risks losing his business credibility with the importer.

# Research the UK Market

**Checklist — Section 1**

1.10    Define and classify the goods to be exported.

1.11    Investigate potential demand for these goods in the UK.

1.12    Investigate quality requirements and acceptable specifications for these goods in the UK.

1.13    Investigate competitive prices for these goods in the UK.

1.14    Investigate UK import duties and any other costs involved within the UK, so that total costs and UK prices can be compared effectively.

1.15    Investigate any restrictions, such as quotas, which may influence the prospects of exporting to the UK, or the timing of export shipments.

1.16    Investigate the most effective means of shipping the goods concerned.

1.17    Investigate UK Health & Safety Regulations, which may affect the goods concerned.

1.18    Investigate ways and means of ensuring satisfactory quality of the goods concerned.

1.19    Investigate names and addresses of potential UK importers.

*Comments*

1.10    Please see Glossary for definition of "goods" and other common

10

*Looking For An Importer.*

and technical terms used in the text. The goods must be classified correctly so they can be described effectively when offered to the UK importer. The UK importer must have a clear idea of what he is being asked to buy and sufficient information to enable him to determine import duties and any import restrictions. These comments may seem self-evident, but accurate and informative descriptions of the goods concerned when first contacting the importer will create a favourable business impression. When necessary, samples dispatched to trade assistance organisations or importers should help to provide information on correct classification. The system of classification used by the UK Customs is the CCCN Classification (Customs Co-operation Council Nomenclature), also commonly known as tariff numbers, e.g. 5802 9000 "Kelem; Schumacks, and Karamanie rugs and the like".

1.11    Sources of commercial information on the UK within the exporter's own country may be found in government-sponsored export promotion centres, whether separate institutions or divisions within Ministries of Commerce or External Trade; Chambers of Commerce, especially when associated with British companies; the British Embassy or High Commission; and international banks with UK connections. Within the UK, apart from business contacts with whom the exporter may already be in touch, the suggested information source is UKTA — The United Kingdom Trade Agency for Developing Countries (see Appendix D for address). This Agency is funded by the Overseas Development Administration, part of the UK Foreign & Commonwealth Office, to assist exporters in developing countries to introduce their goods into the UK market. The information sources given above also apply to items 1.12, 1.13, 1.14, 1.15, 1.17 and 1.19.

1.12    A source of information could be an appropriate UK importer, to whom the exporter supplies samples of goods. UKTA and trade publications may also be of assistance. However, for many types of manufactured goods, the exporter may be able to obtain detailed specifications from the British Standards Institution (see Appendix D for address).

1.13    In commodities, there are many independent sources of price information. The commodity exporter might consult the *Public Ledger* — published daily in the UK. Prices of non-basic commodity articles will require more research. The International Trade Centre in Geneva has published a handbook entitled "Sources of Commodity and Produce Price Information", which provides a list of publications giving price information. For manufactured goods, a British importer or relevant trade publications may be the best source of information.

1.14    If the UK price information which the exporter is able to obtain consists of wholesale prices, then he will need to know costs such as import duties, import handling and transport costs, wholesalers' profit margins, etc., which he will have to add on to his CIF export price in order to make a comparison. The exporter should pay particular attention to import duties as favourable treatment under GSP, or as a Lomé/ACP country, may give him a competitive advantage over some traditional external suppliers of the UK market.

1.15    Quota restrictions are of two kinds: physical quotas which restrict the quantity of goods that can be imported, and tariff or EEC preferential levy quotas which restrict the quantity of goods which can be imported at a preferential rate of duty or levy (see Appendix on Tariff Quotas). For example, in the case of the MFA (Multi-Fibre Arrangement) on many textile goods, it will not be possible to export to the UK once the quota is filled. For some goods, the GSP (see Glossary) preferential rate of duty may be restricted by quota. The goods concerned may still be exported after this type of quota is exhausted, but the full rate of duty will be payable by the importer. As the quota period is normally set from the commencement of the calendar year, then in the case of goods where the quota may be rapidly exhausted, it is prudent to export at the beginning of the year.

1.16    The exporter should seek information and quotations from forwarding agents established in his country. Such firms will be a major source of information on the technical aspects of exporting relating to transportation and documentation. The most effective means of shipment will not necessarily be the cheapest. An obvious example is where expensive air freight has to be used for perishable goods.

1.17    UK health regulations will primarily concern food and agricultural products. The exporter is referred to the Imported Food Regulations implemented under the Food and Drugs Act of 1955. Copies of the regulations can be obtained from Her Majesty's Stationery Office (HMSO) — see Appendix D for the address. These regulations lay down general guidelines which are interpreted and supervised by the Public Health Analyst in the locality concerned, whose job it is to protect the public from harmful products and substances. With regard to certain sensitive manufactured articles, such as electrical equipment and children's toys, there are specific statutory regulations under the Public Safety Act to which the articles concerned must conform. Copies of these regulations can be obtained from HMSO (see Appendix D).

1.18    Once the correct quality specification has been established, the exporter must ensure that his goods match the quality required and also that he has the means to maintain quality. It is no use starting off with the export of goods of satisfactory quality followed by a decline in quality in subsequent shipments. This is the surest way for an exporter to lose his reputation. Importers are now frequently requiring inspection of goods before shipment by independent companies offering inspection and quality-control services. These companies are usually employed by the importer, but the exporter may gain goodwill by offering to permit his goods to be inspected by such a company.

1.19    Names and addresses of trade contacts may be obtained from appropriate trade directories and publications. Copies of such publications may be found in export-promotion centres or Chambers of Commerce and may be had direct from the publishers. UKTA may supply details, including publishers' names and addresses, of such publications.

# Check Export Costs

**Checklist – Section 2**

2.10    Check cost of goods. If buying them elsewhere, obtain firm offer if possible.

2.11    Check packing costs, if any.

2.12    Check packaging costs, if relevant.

2.13    Check transport costs to port/airport.

2.14    Check port costs.

2.15    Check documentation costs and charges.

2.16    Check shipping or freight costs, including forwarding/shipping agents' charges.

2.17    Check insurance costs, if relevant.

2.18    Check possible interest charges.

2.19    Check possible bank charges.

2.20    Consider profit margin.

*Comments*

2.10    If the exporter is buying his goods elsewhere rather than producing them himself, he should check carefully the supplier's price. He

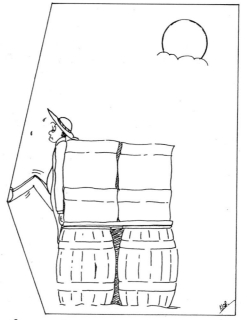

GETTING THE GOODS TO PORT.

should try to obtain the supplier's agreement to offer at a fixed price during the period the exporter will be negotiating his export transaction with the UK importer. He should also try to ensure that he will have a regular supply of the goods concerned for the sake of business continuity.

2.11   The supplier may supply the goods in packing unsuitable for export. If the exporter cannot persuade the supplier to undertake the required packing, he will have to re-pack the goods. He should allow for this cost or any other packing costs. Packing materials must be acceptable to the importer. The latter may specify new jute bags, corrugated cartons, etc., as a formal part of the business contract. Export packing must protect the goods from all likely damage during transit and also be suitable for the easy processing and/or onwards sale of the goods by the importer. Badly packed goods leading to loss or damage would be grounds for claim for reimbursement.

2.12    The terms "packing" and "packaging" should be distinguished. Packing refers to the outer container, e.g. bag, carton, drum, which retains and protects the goods during transit. Packaging generally refers to the wrapping of individual items of the goods concerned and its main purpose is to facilitate sale to the individual consumer. For instance, a kitchen kettle may be packaged in a gaily-printed cardboard box, a can of fruit will be encircled with a multi-coloured label. The importer may specify packaging of his own design and the cost of this, or any other packaging costs, will form part of the cost of the goods. The exporter should note that there are statutory regulations in the UK governing the labelling of many kinds of goods which are to be sold direct to the consumer. Where relevant, the exporter should seek advice on this matter. Copies of regulations can be obtained from HMSO (see Appendix D).

2.13    The exporter must allow for the cost of transporting the goods from the point of supply to the port/airport, etc., from which they will be exported. It will be more economic to transport in full vehicle loads rather than partial vehicle loads. This means the exporter should try to make his offers in quantities related to economic unit loads. This factor is also important to the UK importer who will frequently request quotations in units of 20-feet containers.

2.14    Any storage costs before shipment must be allowed for in calculating total costs. There will also be port charges for receiving and handling the goods.

2.15    Invoices certified by a Chamber of Commerce and/or Commercial Consulate are not required when importing into the UK but may be needed for other countries. In such circumstances, the cost of certifying invoices must be taken into account. However, when exporting to the UK, it is highly likely that either GSP Form A or EUR 1 Form will need to be supplied in order to obtain preferential tariff treatment for the goods. The exporter may have to supply shipping documents (both negotiable originals and copies) for which there may be small charges. Depending upon the type of goods, the importer may require the exporter to supply him with various certificates such as a weight certificate (confirming the weight of the goods), certificate of analysis (confirming the quality or specification of the goods), a certificate of fumigation (confirming the goods have been protected against insect infestation), etc. For textiles subject to the MFA (see Glossary), an export licence will be required. The expense of obtaining certifications may well prove significant.

 2.16    An exporter may directly approach a shipping line, airline, etc., to find out the cost of transporting his goods to the UK, or any other country. However, in view of the considerable amount of expertise that is required in checking the best means of shipment, overseeing the procedures for handling and loading the goods at the port/airport, obtaining necessary documents involved in shipping the goods and negotiating payment (and ensuring that they are free from errors which could prove costly), the exporter would be advised to employ a sound forwarding, freight or receiving agent. These terms are generally interchangeable and henceforth the term "forwarding agent" only will be employed. The forwarding agent, when advising on the most economic means of shipment, will have to take into account the speed and reliability of shipment. The importer will generally require the goods to arrive by a certain date in his country and, for this reason, the exporter may have to use a more expensive "liner conference" shipping service which guarantees regular shipments, rather than a cheaper "non-conference service". The forwarding agent normally charges a percentage of the freight costs for his services and may also make itemised charges for special services such as obtaining documents and certificates, which will be additional to the actual cost of such documents and certificates. In some countries, the forwarding agent may receive a small commission from the shipping line, etc., for introducing the exporter's business and this may be taken into account in determining the forwarding agent's fees.

2.17    If the exporter is undertaking the shipment of the goods, the importer may require him to insure them against loss or damage during shipment, depending upon whether the business contract terms are C&F on the one hand or CIF and Delivered Duty Paid on the other. The cost of such insurance, if applicable to the exporter, must be added to his total costs. It is usual for UK importers to request insurance of the goods at up to 10% above cost including freight. This provides the importer with a legitimate margin if he has to replace the goods in the event of loss. If the contract terms are C&F, insurance is the responsibility of the importer. The exporter is only responsible for ensuring the goods are shipped correctly, but not for any loss or damage incurred during the voyage (see Section 6).

2.18    The exporter may have to borrow money to finance his export transaction. Interest charges on borrowed money should represent part of the overall cost. Even if the exporter does not have to borrow money to finance the transaction but is able to employ his own funds, the notional interest he might have earned on such funds should be taken into account in determining overall costs.

2.19    Depending upon the type of transaction and payment terms, the exporter will probably be involved in various bank charges, as for instance covering the cost of handling shipping documents and submitting these to the importer's bank, negotiating payment, converting the importer's payment draft into local currency, charges for cables, telexes, postage, etc., incurred by his bank on his behalf. The total of these costs can frequently make a significant difference to the exporter's net profit margin and the new exporter may fail to take them into account (see Sections 6 and 7).

2.20    After investigating and checking all potential costs, the exporter must decide upon a reasonable profit margin to recompense him for undertaking the export transaction. This margin should be added to his total costs in order to determine the price at which he will offer his goods. The size of the profit margin will be limited by competitive forces. The exporter cannot normally charge more than the price at which his competitors are able to offer similar goods to the importer with whom he is transacting business. This means that, in the last analysis, the exporter's profit margin will largely depend upon his ability to ensure his costs are satisfactorily below the price determined by competition, unless lack of alternative suppliers enables him to impose his own price on the importer.

However, it must be emphasised that in many instances a new supplier will have difficulty in entering the market unless he is prepared to offer his goods at a discount on the price offered by established suppliers. The exporter has to persuade the importer that he is a reliable supplier of sound quality goods. This can only be really proved by undertaking a number of business transactions. The importer may only be prepared to accept the risk of doing business with a new supplier if he is given the financial incentive of a cheaper price. Once the exporter has established the reliability of his supply and the quality of his goods, he should be in the position to negotiate a better price.

# Make Business Contact

**Checklist — Section 3**

3.10  Draw up list of names and addresses of potential business contacts.

3.11  Decide on method of communication.

3.12  Ensure availability of samples and/or sales catalogues and price lists.

3.13  Make initial communication(s).

3.14  Consider response(s).

*Comments*

3.10  The exporter will have investigated sources of names and addresses of potential business contacts (see Section 1). He should draw up a list of those importers he believes are most likely to conduct business with him. This will not normally be an easy task due to the new exporter's initial lack of knowledge of the UK market. Trade directories may be out of date, businesses may have changed their area of activities or ceased trading, and accessible published information may give little indication of the size and experience of the importers listed.

3.11  If possible, the exporter should use English as the language of communication when dealing with the UK market. Familiarity with other languages is not widespread. The exporter has the choice of approaching potential importers initially by cable, telex or letter. On the whole, letter is preferable for an initial approach, while cable and telex might be employed once business contact has been estab-

Making Contact.

lished. The exporter should take care his correspondence creates a good impression by ensuring that the paper is of good quality, letterheadings well printed, the letter content concise and free from grammatical errors and misuse of words. In addition to writing direct to a number of potential importers, the exporter may signify his interest in making business contacts by placing a notice in a relevant UK trade association circular, or possibly by advertising in trade publications. Free notices can be placed in the British Importers Confederation's (BIC) *Trade Opportunities* supplement. Chambers of Commerce circulars to their members, such as the London Chamber of Commerce & Industry's fortnightly publication "Openings for Trade", also generally accept trade enquiry notices without charge. Alternatively, the exporter might decide to make a personal visit to the UK to meet potential contacts before undertaking any trade. Generally, however, he should be able to carry out initial business transactions without personal contact.

3.12  The UK importer will require samples and/or sales catalogues and price lists to assist him in deciding whether to ask for an offer or place an order. Samples of commodities and small manufactured articles may be sent by air parcel post comparatively inexpensively. The maximum weight will depend upon the postal regulations of the sending country. However, it is unlikely to be more than 20 kilos at the most. They should be well packed to prevent damage. Sending samples by air freight may or may not cost more, but the importer will be reluctant to receive samples in this way, unless he has specifically requested, because of the high handling costs for which he will be normally responsible when the goods reach the UK. Samples should always conform to the quality of the goods being offered to the importer. Exporting goods below the quality of the samples will destroy the exporter's business reputation, and could be grounds for rejecting the shipment. Catalogues should be well printed and in good English. If necessary, professional translators should be employed. Care and attention must be paid to drafting the catalogue. A badly-printed and inaccurately-worded catalogue will create a poor impression which may hinder the development of business. However, a good catalogue can be a very powerful business aid. The same remarks apply to price lists.

3.13  The exporter can make his initial communication with a potential importer without enclosing samples and/or catalogues and wait for the importer to request them. This limited approach may be justified to save the expense of sending samples/catalogues, particularly if the exporter is uncertain whether the contact is likely to be interested in his products. However, it will normally save time to enclose small samples and/or catalogue with the first letter. Generally, this will make the approach seem more businesslike. Of course, the exporter through his initial research should try to ensure that he only approaches importers likely to do business with him. Unfortunately, it is often far from easy to determine such contacts in advance, as already mentioned.

3.14    The potential importer may respond negatively to the exporter's approach. He may inform the exporter that his price(s) are uncompetitive and/or that the quality of his goods is unsatisfactory. The exporter will then have to consider whether any changes are possible. On the whole, the exporter can expect the UK importer to be generally interested in developing new trade contacts and to provide him with constructive information. There will, of course, be exceptions to the rule. If the response is favourable, then the exporter goes on to the next stages of preparing and undertaking a specific export transaction.

# Prepare to Export

4.10   Check whether any changes required in the specification of the goods.

4.11   Make a final check on costs, including any changes resulting from modifications requested in the specification of the goods.

4.12   Check the quantity and quality of goods available for delivery.

4.13   Check time taken for delivery to the UK.


*Comments*

4.10   The specification of the exporter's goods may be accepted unaltered by the importer. On the other hand, the importer may request some changes. In this case, the exporter must determine whether they are major or minor. Major changes may require product development, changes in design, etc., which will take time and investment to implement. The exporter will, therefore, have to consider delaying the export transaction he has planned, perhaps for some considerable time. If the changes can be remedied quickly, such as an alteration in packaging, better grading and selection, etc., then the exporter may be able to go ahead with an export transaction without significant delay and proceed to the next stages.

4.11   The exporter should always be on the lookout for last-minute changes in costs which might involve him in a loss if he goes ahead and agrees to sell his goods to the importer at a price previously considered as satisfactory.

"Hey!... You Promised to Sell to Me!"

4.12    It would be damaging for the exporter to accept an order and then find he has insufficient goods to meet it. In most cases, the exporter should inform the importer as early as possible in his business negotiations of the quantity of goods he has available to offer. This will prevent misunderstandings and save the exporter from having to admit that he is unable to supply the quantity of goods the importer requires. It will also give the importer time to look around for additional customers if the quantity of goods available is greater than he normally handles, thus enabling him to place a larger order.

4.13    The UK importer will want to know the time that will elapse between placing an order, or accepting an offer, and the arrival of the goods in the UK. This information will enable him to schedule the timing of his imports in relation to his own or his customers' needs. Late delivery will generally be regarded as a very serious matter by the UK importer and, therefore, the exporter must check very carefully his source of supply, availability of internal transportation, vessel departure dates and voyage times, so as to ensure he does not mislead the importer and risk his business reputation and a possible claim for damages.

# Negotiate the Export Transaction

**Checklist – Section 5**

5.10    Determine profit margin and price of goods.

5.11    Determine quotation currency.

5.12    Check possible shipment dates.

5.13    Decide on acceptable terms, for supply and delivery of the goods (see Section 6).

5.14    Decide on acceptable payment terms for the goods (see Section 7).

5.15    Give quotation/offer/price list, if not already submitted, or confirm or modify any price list previously submitted.

5.16    Negotiate any changes in the suggested transaction terms, if necessary.

5.17    Issue contract note, supply note, invoice, letter, etc., to importer confirming the transaction.

*Comments*

5.10    In determining the price for his goods, the exporter will normally add a profit margin to the cost. A profit margin represents profit in percentage terms of the total costs. The size of the profit margin will depend upon the exporter's costs and competitive conditions in the UK market. The exporter may find it necessary to undercut the prices offered by the competitors in order to establish his goods

NEGOTIATION.

in the UK market. This will result in a lower profit margin than he might have otherwise obtained. If the price only permits an unacceptably low margin of profit after taking into account costs, or even more so if the price is below the exporter's costs, he will naturally have to consider carefully before undertaking the business. Nevertheless, the exporter may be prepared to sell initially at a loss providing he is more or less certain that prices can be raised to a profitable level later (see 2.20).

5.11    When giving his price, the exporter will have to decide on the currency he wishes to employ. International trade tends to be conducted in a limited number of major currencies, such as US dollars, pounds sterling, German marks, etc. His own country's currency is likely to be unacceptable to the importer as a means of quoting prices, though the exporter's costs will be largely in terms of his own currency. The exporter, therefore, should choose an acceptable currency which he believes will remain stable or possibly appreciate in terms of his own currency. In this way, he will seek to avoid any losses due to converting a foreign currency into his own when he receives payment. UK importers will ideally prefer quotations in pounds sterling, but quotations in US dollars or other major international currencies will be generally acceptable. In some countries, regulations may permit the exporter to cover his currency risk by selling the foreign currency in the Forward Exchange Market.

5.12    When negotiating a transaction, the exporter must be in the position to advise the UK importer when he can expect the goods to arrive. He should also be prepared to advise on frequency of possible future shipments, so the importer can plan repeat orders.

5.13    The exporter must make up his mind on the terms under which he will be selling and delivering his goods. Such terms can be divided basically into those which are concerned with the physical aspects of supplying and delivering the goods to the importer, and those concerned with payment for the goods. In some commodity trades, there are standard international contract terms which the exporter will generally have to accept without alteration. Such standard printed contracts often set forth in great detail the obligations of each trading partner, and the procedure to be followed in the event of failure to fulfil the contract terms. However, for most goods, including general manufactures, the contractual responsibilities of each trading partner are unlikely to be set forth in detail, although all the basic essentials of the transaction must be noted. Where terms and conditions are not openly stated, they will be assumed to be the same as normal business practice. Stated terms and conditions involving the supply and delivery of goods for export are likely to involve some or all of the following items:
(a) Price of goods.
(b) Quantity of goods.
(c) Quality of goods.
(d) Packing of goods.

(e)  Packaging of goods.

(f)  Date of availability/shipment/arrival/delivery of goods in UK, depending upon the terms of shipment agreed (see Section 6).

(g)  Means of shipment.

(h)  Destination of shipment; a clear statement by means of established standard shipping terms of the place in the movement of the goods where delivery ceases to be the responsibility of the exporter and becomes the importer's responsibility (see Glossary — Trade Terms).

(i)  Documents to be supplied/required by exporter/importer (see Sections 6 and 7).

(j)  Insurance cover.

(k)  Settlement of any disputes resulting from the transaction.

A forwarding agent should be able to help in advising on contract terms and documentation concerning the delivery of the goods.

5.14    In addition to the delivery of the goods to the importer, the exporter must also consider terms of payment, that is how he is going to receive payment for the goods he has sold to the importer. The exporter will be concerned to arrange payment terms involving least risk of non-payment by the importer, and will also want payment as soon as possible. The importer, however, might wish to delay paying until after the goods are in his possession and have been sold on to his customers. A major bank will generally be able to advise on suitable payment terms (see Glossary and Section 7).

5.15    The exporter may have already given an indication of prices at the time of his initial contact with the importer. However, at this stage he should now have a firm idea of the price(s) which will form part of his business transaction with the importer. In commodity trading there is generally a crucial difference between the term "quotation" and the term "offer". The word "offer" is employed by the exporter to make a firm commitment from which he cannot withdraw if the importer accepts within a specified time period. The use of the word "quotation", on the other hand, does not bind the exporter. Outside commodity trading the use of terms is more flexible. The exporter will normally use terms such as: we quote/

our price/as per our price list/etc., to indicate what he wishes the importer to pay. The exporter would be free to change his price until the stage when he has confirmed the importer's order.

5.16    In order for a transaction to be concluded the terms must be mutually acceptable to both parties, the exporter and the importer. This means that after one side has first stated his terms, usually the seller (exporter), the other has the right to negotiate changes. Disagreement can occur in any area, but may most frequently happen over price, shipment dates, payment terms and the kinds of documents required.

5.17    The buyer (importer) eventually affirms his agreement to buy. The seller (exporter) will then normally give some document confirming his agreement to the transaction. If the exporter is inexperienced, the importer may take the initiative and issue a contract note. In general manufactured goods, the exporter may confirm the transaction in various ways, partly dependent upon the payment terms. For instance, he might issue a simple commercial invoice if payment is being made direct by the importer. However, such a method of payment will only usually be employed when the exporter and importer are well known to each other as it provides little protection to the exporter. He may draw a Bill of Exchange for the importer to sign if this is the method of payment. He may issue a supply note — this is a simplified form of contract note — or just a letter or telex confirming his goods will be delivered on the terms negotiated or agreed. All means of confirmation, even a telex, should re-state the main features of the transaction.

# Shipment of Goods

### Checklist — Section 6

6.10   Check details of contract/order note/Letter of Credit, etc., and/or any other instructions from the importer concerning supply and shipment of the goods concerned. Make certain that there are no discrepancies between any instructions received from the importer, and what the exporter believes has been contractually agreed. If there are discrepancies, these must be clarified as soon as possible, and certainly before shipment.

6.11   Ensure goods are delivered to the port/airport, etc., well in time for the date of shipment agreed with the importer.

6.12   Check all goods concerned are correct in all respects and are suitably packed for shipment. This may include loading into containers.

6.13   Ensure packing is marked with agreed shipping marks.

6.14   If responsible for shipment to importer's country, check all details with forwarding agent including any changes in shipping schedules.

6.15   Make sure forwarding agent has booked the goods on a suitable boat/aircraft as agreed with the importer.

6.16   Arrange insurance during shipment, if responsible.

6.17   Ensure all pre-shipment requirements such as provision of certificates of analysis, weight certificates, certificates of fumigation, provision of pre-shipment samples, etc., are undertaken in good time before shipment.

MISSING THE BOAT.

6.18    Prepare or obtain all shipment documentation such as Bills of Lading, invoices, etc., required by the importer and/or his bankers, and check all such documentation is correct.

6.19    If export licences are required, these must be obtained in good time.

6.20    Check shipment has been made.

6.21    Ensure all shipping and other documents required for clearing the goods on arrival in the UK reach the importer or his bank in good time so that the goods can be cleared without delay.

### Comments

6.10    The importance of checking and re-checking all the contractual terms of the export transaction cannot be over-emphasised. Misunderstandings between the exporter and importer can easily arise. The exporter may believe that he has agreed certain terms and conditions with the importer, and then discover on careful reading of the contract note/order note/Letter of Credit, etc., issued by the importer, that there are still differences to be settled. Especial attention must be paid to the wording of Letters of Credit, L/C (see Glossary) issued on behalf of the importer by his bank. If the instructions it contains are not adhered to rigidly, then the bank may legitimately refuse payment for the goods, and the exporter will find himself entirely dependent upon the goodwill of the importer to receive payment. For instance, the L/C may prohibit transhipment of the goods (see Glossary) — that is transferring the goods from one vessel to another at an intermediate stage during the shipment — and presenting a Bill of Lading showing the goods would be transhipped would be sufficient grounds for the bank to refuse payment under the L/C.

However, the most likely issue will be the expiry date of the L/C, when it ceases to be valid. The exporter must have sufficient time to carry out the terms of the contract specified under the L/C, such as shipping the goods and sending the required documents to the importer's bank. If the exporter does not believe that he has sufficient time, he must ask the exporter to extend the expiry date of the L/C, and, prudently, should withhold shipment until he receives confirmation of the extension. Naturally, as the exporter and importer become accustomed to trading with each other, the chances of misunderstanding should be reduced. The exporter must always be careful to protect his position by giving the importer no cause for complaint which would enable him to withhold payment.

6.11  Delivery of goods on time will be a very important condition in most export transactions, and failure to deliver on time may open the exporter to claims for damages. In view of this, the exporter must make every effort to ensure the goods reach the port in time for the scheduled shipment.

6.12  If the exporter is purchasing from an outside supplier, he must be careful to check that the goods are completely in accordance with the quantity and quality he has contracted to supply to the importer. He is responsible to the importer, and it is no use the exporter trying to blame the supplier for any deficiencies. The importer may also have requested specific packing, e.g. new jute bags, fibre-board drums, etc., and the exporter must ensure he receives the goods from his supplier packed accordingly, or he will have to repack them. The importer may also specify shipment in standard 20-feet containers and/or on pallets, and the exporter must make sure that such containers and/or pallets are available in good time for receiving his goods before shipment on the vessel concerned.

6.13 The importer may frequently require that bales, bags, cartons, etc., are marked in such a manner that they can be easily identified by those handling the goods on arrival at the port and in his warehouse. These are called "shipping marks" and must be clearly legible and resistant to removal.

6.14 Whether the exporter is responsible for shipment or not will depend upon the shipping terms agreed in the export contract (see Glossary). If he has sold FOB the exporter will not be responsible for shipment to the importer's country. His responsibility will be limited to ensuring the goods are available for loading in good time on board the vessel or aircraft nominated by the importer. If he has contracted C&F, CIF or DDP (Delivered Duty Paid to the importer's premises), then he will be responsible for shipment. In such cases, the exporter must ensure that the information he gives to the importer on shipping dates is correct. If the vessel concerned is delayed for one reason or another, then he must advise the importer immediately. Normally, the importer may accept late shipment if he believes the exporter is genuinely not responsible. However, he may have the option to refuse the goods or claim damages.

6.15 If the export transaction is C&F, CIF or DDP, the exporter must ensure in good time that there is space available on the vessel concerned. His forwarding agent will normally take on the task of "booking" the goods in an agreed vessel. If the contract terms are

DDP, then the forwarding agent will also make arrangements to ensure the goods are cleared through the destination port and Customs, that Duty, if any, is paid, and the goods are delivered onwards to the importer's warehouse. Exchange control regulations in developing countries may prevent exporters offering DDP contracts.

6.16    The exporter will be responsible for insurance of the goods if he undertakes export on a CIF or DDP (see Glossary – Trade Terms). Although on a CIF basis he is only strictly required to insure the goods up to discharge from the vessel at the destination port, he may be requested to extend the insurance cover to the importer's warehouse. If any loss or damage occurs during shipment, the importer will require him to claim against the insurance company on his behalf. However, it is possible for the exporter to endorse the insurance policy into the name of the importer thus allowing the importer himself to claim. Under a C&F contract, the exporter is responsible for shipping the goods, but not insuring them. In this case, he must supply the importer with information, such as the vessel's name and sailing date, to enable the importer to insure the goods himself. It is not unusual to insure the goods for up to 10% above contract value to recompense the importer for the cost of having to replace the goods concerned. Although a C&F contract does not require the exporter to insure the goods, he has a contingent insurable interest in case the importer fails to insure, and then refuses to pay for the goods if a loss occurs during shipment. He should ensure that the importer has a valid insurance policy, or cover for this contingency risk, for which the premium is generally low, by taking out a contingency insurance policy.

6.17    The importer may set certain contract conditions to protect himself, as far as possible, against shipment of goods which do not meet the contract terms on quantity and/or quality. These may require the exporter to have his goods checked by independent surveyors or a surveillance company to establish that the weights are correct and/ or select pre-shipment samples, to provide a certificate of analysis of the composition of the goods from a firm of analysts, to employ a specialist enterprise in fumigation to protect the goods concerned against insect infestation, etc. The exporter may be required to supply certificates from these organisations as part of his contractual documentation. The cost of obtaining such certificates will normally be borne by the exporter. However, importers themselves are frequently employing specialist companies in the exporter's country to undertake pre-shipment inspection and quality control.

6.18   The documentation which the exporter will have to prepare will depend upon the terms of payment (see Section 7), and the method of transport, i.e. Bills of Lading for ships, Air Waybills for aircraft, etc. (see Glossary). A basic document is the commercial invoice, which is a claim for payment for the goods sold. Even if a commercial invoice is not expressly demanded as part of the payment terms, either a commercial invoice or a pro forma invoice will be required for clearing the goods through UK Customs. A pro forma invoice gives the same details of quality of goods, description of goods and cost of goods to the importer as a commercial invoice, but is not a demand for payment. The invoice, which is the basic document for clearance through Customs, does not normally have to be certified by a local Chamber of Commerce or Consular authorities when exporting to the UK, in contrast to many other countries where such certification is required.

The other type of basic document is the transport document. This may be a document of title such as Bill of Lading or a non-titular document such as a Forwarding Agent's Receipt. The difference between these two types of shipping documents is that a document of title transfers ownership of the goods listed on it as well as signifying shipment of the goods, while a non-titular shipping document only signifies receipt or shipment. In such cases, ownership is transferred under the terms of the contract and by ensuring the goods are placed physically at the disposal of the importer.

The contract terms, particularly where Letters of Credit are involved, will often specify how many copies of invoices and shipping documents are required, and these details must be strictly followed. Special export documents which the importer may require may include an export licence or certificate in the case of textile goods subject to the Multi-Fibre Arrangement, and GSP Form A or EUR 1 for preferential import duty treatment. With the limited exception of some Centrally Planned Economies, all developing countries receive preferential tariff treatment, and in the case of ACP/Lomé countries and "Least Developed Countries" (LLDCs), the great majority of their products can enter the UK duty free. A limited list of products, such as live animals, hides and skins from endangered species, etc., may require a special export certificate before the importer can obtain a licence to import the goods into the UK. Otherwise, virtually all categories of goods can be imported into the UK under an "Open General Licence" which means the UK importer does not require permission to import (see Glossary).

6.19   Some countries may require exporters to obtain licences for a limited or wide range of goods before shipment will be permitted. If the exporter is selling FOB, the importer will require him to obtain the appropriate licence. The exporter should ensure that his contract with the importer does not leave him liable for damages if he fails to obtain the export licence. In the case of textile goods subject to the MFA, export licences will be required by the importer in order to obtain an import licence to import into the UK.

6.20   It is easy for the exporter to assume that his goods have been shipped at the due time on the vessel he has nominated when, in fact, this is not the case. The exporter should check that shipment has taken place as the vessel might have failed to arrive as expected, while his forwarding agent may have omitted to inform him. Sometimes the available cargo space on a vessel may be over-booked and the exporter will find his goods "shut out", that is left on the quayside unshipped (see Glossary).

6.21   If the importer or his agent does not have the documents required for clearing the goods through Customs or handling them through the destination port, he is likely to be involved in additional clearance charges. For instance, if the Bills of Lading do not arrive in time, the importer may not be able to clear his goods through the port from the quayside. If Bills of Lading arrive after the vessel arrives these are called "stale bills". This could enable the importer to refuse to accept the goods under the terms of the contract, thus involving the exporter in considerable potential expense. Even if he accepts the goods he will have the right to ask the exporter to pay additional costs such as penalty charges for failing to clear the goods concerned from the quayside within the limited period allowed.

# Payment for Goods

**Checklist – Section 7**

7.10    Check commercial and financial soundness of prospective importer.

7.11    Negotiate and agree, in conjunction with the other terms and conditions of the business transaction, the payment method for the goods (see 5.16 and 5.18).

7.12    Give instructions and prepare documents necessary for receiving payment.

7.13    Check all activities for obtaining payment are proceeding satisfactorily.

7.14    Check payment has been received.

7.15    If necessary, change foreign currency into local currency.

(These steps will be largely taken in conjunction with those outlined in Section 6.)

*Comments*

7.10    It is prudent to check the business soundness of a potential importer as early as possible when considering an export transaction. Obviously if the information received is unsatisfactory, it will be advisable not to proceed further because of the risk. Whenever deciding upon payment terms, the exporter should have some idea of the financial standing of the importer with whom he is intending to deal as this will have an important bearing on the terms the

Goods Against Payment.

exporter will regard as acceptable. For instance, he may feel that there is little risk of not receiving payment from a major enterprise with a long-established reputation in international trade. On the other hand, he may be concerned about the possibility of non-payment by a small importer who has only been trading for a short time.

The usual method of checking is for the exporter to ask his bank to approach the importer's bank for information. For this reason, it is perfectly legitimate for the exporter to request the prospective importer for the name of his bank, and the importer may be surprised if he does not do so. Further sources of information may be friendly businesses familiar with the importer concerned, or the services of a suitable credit enquiry agency. The exporter must always bear in mind that it will be difficult and costly to undertake legal proceedings in a distant country

Some of the more industrialised developing countries have 'export credit' insurance schemes which enable the exporter to insure against non payment in defined circumstances. The exporter should consider taking advantage of such schemes if they are available.

7.11   There is a wide range of payment methods and the choice will reflect the desire of both exporter and importer to minimise their commercial risks. The exporter has an interest in obtaining secure and prompt payment for his goods. The importer has an interest in ensuring he receives the correct quantity and quality of goods at the time he has stipulated, and may wish to hold up payment until he is certain these conditions have been met. The objective is to find payment terms which are mutually satisfactory to both parties. At the outset, both exporter and importer are more likely to be suspicious of each other's intentions than after they have been trading together for some time. Consequently, in initial transactions, payment terms are likely to be hedged with precautions and conditions which may be dispensed with at a later stage. The advice of banks should be sought on suitable payment terms. The major possibilities are itemised as follows:

(a)   By sending a commercial invoice and shipping documents (if required) direct to the importer without any precautions. This implies the exporter trusts the importer to pay in due course when he has received the goods, or documents, whichever has been agreed. This is called an "open account" transaction.

(b)   By requiring the importer to accept a Bill of Exchange. As a result of accepting a Bill of Exchange (see Glossary), the importer makes non-payment potentially very damaging as an accepted Bill of Exchange is an internationally recognised legal claim for the sum of money concerned.

(c)   By negotiating the principal documents such as the commercial invoice and the Bills of Lading through a bank. This generally means that the importer cannot obtain possession of the goods until he has paid. This is called a "collection payment". There are internationally recognised commercial rules for collection payments entitled "Uniform Rules for Collections". Copies of these rules may be obtained from a local chamber of commerce or bank. This method of payment is commonly referred to as "Cash against Documents" (CAD) and is very frequently employed, being less expensive and more flexible than the Documentary Letter of Credit described next under item (d). It does not, however, provide the same protection for the exporter against non-payment.

(d) By Documentary Letter of Credit (L/C) negotiated through a bank. This generally means that the exporter is assured of payment by the importer's bank before the goods are shipped, although actual payment will not normally take place until after the goods have been shipped. (See Glossary for fuller description of these terms.) Rules and conditions for Documentary Credits are established internationally under the title "Uniform Customs and Practice for Documentary Credits", which may be found with local chambers of commerce, banks, etc. Some developing countries may insist that all exports be undertaken on L/C terms, because this method of payment is easiest to control against breaches in Exchange Control regulations.

7.12    Instructions to banks and forwarding agents and preparation of documents will depend upon the method of payment chosen. Generally speaking, the new exporter is likely to be using the banking system to help ensure he receives payment. In the case of a L/C, he will first agree with the importer the terms of the Letter of Credit. The importer will then instruct his bank (the opening bank) to open a L/C in favour of the exporter. The exporter will then instruct his bank, or possibly his forwarding agent, to present the documents required under the terms of the L/C to the opening bank. Often, the importer will agree to the negotiation of the L/C in the exporter's country through a local bank (correspondent bank) appointed by the opening bank. The exporter may then be able to present documents and negotiate the L/C personally with the correspondent bank, thus saving on time and bank charges. However, if he has borrowed money to finance his export, the exporter's bank may wish to retain the shipping documents in its own custody as collateral against the loan, and will negotiate the documents with the correspondent bank in order to receive payment itself. Letters of Credit generally provide the strictest form of payment method for protecting the conflicting interests of exporter and importer, but at the cost of significant bank charges.

If the exporter is not selling under a L/C, he may still obtain payment from the importer before losing control of his goods by sending the shipping documents to a bank in the importer's country and asking the importer to collect the documents from the bank against payment. The importer will normally be able to inspect the documents to see if they are correct, but the bank will hold them in trust and not surrender them until payment has been received. Without the shipping documents, the importer will not be able to gain possession of the goods. Alternatively, the goods may be consigned to a forwarding agent in the UK who will have instructions not to release the goods until he is assured that payment has been received. In this case, the UK forwarding agent would normally oversee the importation of the goods. There are many options available for controlling payment from the importer when the exporter is doubtful about his reliability. Generally speaking, UK importers can be expected to meet their obligations, but there will be exceptions to the rule, and the inexperienced exporter should seek advice from his forwarding agent and bank on how best to protect his interests.

7.13    The exporter may believe that everything is going well, and that payment will be received as arranged in due course. However, if shipping documents are being sent overseas in order to negotiate payment, there may be unexpected delays in their arrival, or, when they arrive, the importer or his bank may refuse to accept them because they are incorrect. Unless such problems are dealt with promptly, the exporter may find himself involved in additional costs and possible claims resulting from receiving the documents after arrival of the vessel. Generally speaking, while banks can be relied upon to carry out specific instructions, it is not usually their responsibility to show initiative when events do not go according to plan. They will expect to receive new instructions, and it can be costly for the exporter to delay in giving these.

7.14    There may also be delays in transmitting the money from overseas to the exporter's own country. The exporter should remain in close contact with his bank to ensure such delays are minimised. The bank also may be slow in converting the foreign currency received into the exporter's local currency.

7.15    In most developing countries exchange control regulations will require that the local bank automatically converts into local currency any foreign currency received for the exporter's account. When the exporter has some discretion in holding foreign currency, then he must make a decision whether to retain it, or convert it into some other currency, possibly his own.

If the exporter has been able to sell the foreign currency he expects to receive from the transaction in the forward currency market, he will then have to close the transaction with the bank concerned by handing over the foreign currency he has received in payment for his goods. Some countries may allow the exporter to sell part of the foreign exchange he earns on a free market basis to local importers requiring such currency to buy goods for import. As currency sold in this way usually commands a premium over the official rate of exchange, this can add to the profitability of exporting. This concession, in fact, is given by the Government as an export incentive.

# Assessment

**Checklist — Section 8**

8.10 Re-check all costs and calculate profit made.

8.11 Assess any difficulties met during the export transaction and decide what measures should be taken to overcome them in future.

8.12 Reconsider all costs and see if savings can be made.

8.13 Assess any action required to increase the supply of goods for future transactions, or improve their quality.

8.14 Plan how business might be developed in the future.

*Comments*

8.10 In the original calculations (see Section 5) many minor expenses may have been omitted. The exporter may have been misinformed about certain costs which turn out to be greater or smaller than expected. A deduction of total costs from the amount received will give the exporter his profit margin. This should be calculated in percentage terms. By this means he will be able to measure the profitability of the current transaction against future transactions and perhaps establish a minimum percentage profit margin which he requires to obtain for continuing in the business concerned.

8.11 The exporter may have had problems in obtaining his goods on time, quality may have been uneven, packing inadequate, his forwarding agent lacking in efficiency, payment may have been received late from the importer, etc. Few export transactions run smoothly, at least at the beginning of new trading.

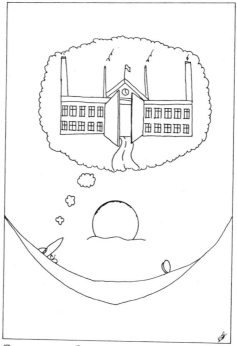

PLANNING FOR THE FUTURE.

8.12    The exporter should go item by item through all the costs involved in each transaction and see if savings might be made. For instance, he might reduce the cost of his goods if he could assure his supplier of regular orders. He should consider trying to persuade the importer to order from him on a regular basis and may offer the incentive of a reduction in price representing a share in the cost saving. He might persuade the importer that some of the documentation and certificates required are unnecessary. He might find it feasible to use cheaper "non-conference" shipping lines in spite of the fact that the sailing dates may be less reliable. The exporter will often find that the UK importer is prepared to co-operate in reducing costs as long as the commercial soundness of the business is not affected. As the UK importer may frequently have greater experience of the trade than the developing country exporter, the latter should be prepared to ask for advice and assistance when this does not conflict with the business interests of the importer.

8.13 If it seems the trade is likely to develop, the exporter may have to take steps to increase the supply of the goods involved. If he is producing them himself, this may mean taking on additional labour and buying more plant and equipment. If he is buying the goods from the outside, then he may have to persuade his supplier to increase production and/or seek new suppliers. He may also have to take long-term measures to improve quality. The exporter should bear in mind that quality improvement is a continuing world-wide phenomenon.

8.14 Every professional businessman should have a plan of how he believes his business should be developed in the future. Such a plan will act as a guide to what he should be doing. Of course, forecasts will prove to be wrong and circumstances will change and the plan will have to be adapted accordingly. In developing his plan the exporter may find himself considering some of the following items:
   (a) When should he visit the UK, assuming he has not already done so?
   (b) What sort of functions does he require the importer to exercise in order to best develop the sales of his goods?
   (c) Should he seek to conduct business with a number of competing UK importers, or try to develop his business exclusively through one?
   (d) If so, what kind of agency agreement would be suitable?
   (e) What UK sales targets should he set in the foreseeable future?
   (f) What kinds of improvements should he consider to his existing goods, and how should these be achieved?
   (g) Should he seek to add other goods to his range of existing exports?
   (h) Should he participate in suitable trade fairs and exhibitions? This will be expensive, but may be the most effective means of developing the market for his goods. If the exporter has an agent, the latter might take on the role of exhibiting his goods at fairs within the country concerned.

# Some Practical Hints and Information

### Programming Appointments

As far as possible the exporter should try to arrange a programme of appointments with business contacts in advance of his visit to the UK. This will save valuable time when he arrives. Due allowance must be made for travelling time between appointments. If the exporter is visiting London, he should remember that London is a large city and it would be impractical to plan more than four appointments in one day unless they are all within a short distance of each other.

### UK Entry Regulations

Visitors from some countries may require a visa to enter the UK. These can be obtained from the UK Diplomatic Missions and major Commercial Consulates. When passing through Immigration Control on entry into the UK, the visitor will be asked the length of his stay in the UK and may also be asked to show that he has sufficient resources to support himself during his visit.

### Trade Samples

Generally speaking, the businessman bringing trade samples of commercial value into the UK for display to his customers will be expected to pay the applicable rate of duty together with Value Added Tax (VAT), which, except principally for food items, is at 15% *ad valorem*. However, a concessionary system is in operation if the samples are limited to one of each category, with some discretion on quantity in the case of articles easily soiled or damaged, provided that they are re-exported from the UK within twelve months. The exporter will be requested to complete a Customs Entry form, either C12 or C10, and will have to deposit the Duty and VAT, which will be refunded when the goods are re-exported. He may, however, come from a country which operates the ATA Carnet system, which would enable him to import his samples into the UK without payment of Duty or VAT. He will be responsible for ensuring the goods are re-exported within the given time period. Otherwise, he will be subject to Duty and VAT which may be deducted from the money he will have to deposit in his own country when he obtained his carnet. The carnet system is usually administered by Chambers of Commerce.

### Health Requirements and Precautions

Generally speaking, there are no health requirements for visitors entering the UK.

In the rare case of countries suffering epidemics, such as cholera, inoculation certificates may be expressly required and the businessman should be notified of this by his travel agent before he leaves his own country. Within the UK tap drinking water is safe and the visitor should not normally need preventive inoculation against any diseases. However, any treatment under the National Health Service or privately will ordinarily be charged, and business visitors might consider taking out health insurance if they are able to do so, and are concerned about medical charges.

## Dress

The English climate is temperate and visitors from tropical countries should bring with them medium-weight woollen or wool mixture suits, except, perhaps, in July and August. Overcoats will be required in the winter. Suits should be worn for business appointments.

## Punctuality

Strict punctuality is expected in appointments. The exporter should arrive on time, but if he is delayed or has to cancel an appointment, he should immediately inform his business contact by telephone. The UK telephone system is on direct dialling, and all numbers can normally be reached quickly without use of the operator.

## Business Meetings

The exporter should generally adopt a friendly, business-like manner. If he enquires about prices and other information from his business contact, he can be reasonably assured that the information he receives will be correct. He should not normally suggest a price for his goods greatly in excess of the level he finally intends to accept. Protracted bargaining on prices may not be appreciated by the UK businessman who wishes to conclude the interview one way or another within a reasonable length of time. Except for major negotiations, an hour may be sufficient to conclude a business discussion. However, it is frequent practice for British businessmen to discuss business deals over lunch. If he is invited to lunch, the exporter should accept.

## Trade Fairs and Exhibitions

Perhaps the best method to investigate the British market is to time a visit to the UK to coincide with a trade fair or exhibition related to the goods the exporter wishes to sell. Such a trade fair will usually include exhibition stands by importing agents and merchants as well as by UK manufacturers. Thus, there will be an opportunity to make a number of useful business contacts in one place, in addition to seeing the full range of goods being offered to the UK market in the sector in which the exporter is interested. Such trade fairs seldom last more than one week and the printed fair catalogue listing the participants and their products will also be a valuable aid to the exporter. Details of trade fairs and exhibitions can be obtained from the Exhibition Bulletin (see Appendix C).

### Business Holidays

Most British businessmen work a five-day week and Saturday and Sunday are holidays. Retail outlets will be open on Saturday for selling, but usually management staff will not be available for appointments on that day. A business trip to the UK in August may be unproductive because potential contacts are likely to be away on holiday. The period between 20th December and 2nd January should also be avoided because of the Christmas and New Year holidays. During the celebration of Easter, which falls on weekends varying annually between the end of March and the middle of April, businesses will be closed on Friday and Monday in the following week. The first and last Mondays in May and the last Monday in August are also National Holidays.

### Business Hours

Business offices in the UK generally start work at 9.00 am or 9.30 am and finish at 5.00 pm or 5.30 pm. Banks open at 9.30 am and close at 3.30 pm. They have been closed at weekends, but some are now considering opening on Saturday mornings. In many of the larger towns there are Bureaux de Change which keep longer hours and are open on Saturdays, and even Sundays in Central London. These will change currency and travellers cheques, though rates may not be as good as those obtainable from banks. Post Offices generally open from 9.00 am until 5.30 pm. Larger offices are also open on Saturday mornings. Retail shops only generally close on Sundays, though there are increasing exceptions to this rule. In larger towns, it is possible to find food shops open after office hours.

### Foreign Exchange

There are no currency restrictions. Visitors can bring in as much currency, including pounds sterling, into the UK as they wish and also take out currency of all denominations.

### Sterling Currency Denominations

The Pound is the standard unit of currency, for which the sign is £. There are £1, £5, £10, £20 and £50 notes. The pound is divided into one hundred pence (100p). There are halfpenny (½p), one penny (1p), two pence (2p), five pence (5p), ten pence (10p), twenty pence (20p), fifty pence (50p) and, from spring 1983, one pound (£1) coins.

### Prices

Prices given in this publication must be regarded as approximate only and refer to prices ruling in the middle of 1982.

### Hotel Accommodation

The cost of hotel accommodation in the UK varies considerably. Modern hotels will have bathrooms/shower cubicles attached to the bedroom. In older buildings, the situation varies but the interiors in most of them have been modernised extensively in recent years to bring them up to an acceptable standard. In London the cost of hotel accommodation depends to some extent on location. Prices in the Central area are more expensive than those further out, but even a distance of only two miles from Piccadilly Circus can mean a large difference in price for equivalent accommodation. Generally speaking, a single bedroom at the cheap end of the market in an old building without bathroom/shower attached might, perhaps, cost as little as £10 per night. Modern 3/4-star accommodation might vary from around £25–45 per night. Luxury hotels can cost considerably more. On the whole, hotel prices will tend to be less outside London, but there is considerable variation and a single bedroom with shower/bathroom in a modern or modernised building is likely to be in the £25–35 per night range. (If a bedroom is shared, cost per head may be significantly cheaper.) Three-star hotels and better will provide TV in the bedroom.

Hotel prices will normally be quoted including the standard Value Added Tax (VAT) of 15% and also a service charge. It is now becoming normal practice not to include the cost of breakfast in room charges, although some hotels still do so. It will generally save time to book hotel accommodation in advance of visiting the UK, but if cost is an important consideration the visitor may find assistance in obtaining the sort of accommodation he can afford by visiting the local tourist office. For instance, a publication entitled "100 Good Value Hotels" is available from the Sales Office, London Tourist Board, 26 Grosvenor Gardens, London SW1W 0DU.

## Meals

The price of meals will vary considerably depending on the quality of the cooking, the surroundings, service offered, etc. If the visitor eats in small, minimum-service restaurants, or American-style "fast-food" outlets, an adequate meal may come to under £2 per head. A substantial meal in an ordinary restaurant is likely to be £5–10 per head, and more if wine or spirits are drunk. Prices in luxury restaurants will be higher.

## Tipping

Generally speaking, there is no standard scale for tipping in the UK. Tips tend to be small and the decision is left to the personal generosity of the visitor. It is suggested that 50p–£1 per night might be left for the chambermaid who tidies the bedroom and makes the bed. A tip of 50p is ample for the porter who carries baggage. Taxi drivers usually expect a tip of around 10% of the taxi fare. Tipping in restaurants will depend to some extent on whether a service charge is included in the price or not. It is becoming the usual practice to include such a charge. On the whole, it is not normal to tip more than 10% of the bill, unless the service is exceptional.

## Taxis

London taxis are equipped with meters and work on a standard tariff system related to distance. A journey will work out at around £1 per mile in Central London. Charges are higher at night and on holidays. Outside London, the taxi may not have a meter and one should ask the charge in advance.

## Public Transport

London has an extensive public transport system, using bus and train. In Central, West and East London, the principal train service is the Underground system, managed by London Transport. However, outside the Central area the system tends to be above ground level. In South London an extensive local network is provided by British Rail. Maps of the Underground system are freely available from stations and it provides a quick means of transportation to locations throughout the inner area. In the Central area stretching from the Tower of London to Earls Court the current charge is either 40p or 70p. Bus services (coloured red) also run throughout the inner area. For the outer suburbs there is a Green Line bus system as well as an extensive rail network.

London is connected with most of the major towns in the UK by a frequent and rapid rail service. Birmingham is about 1½ hours by rail from London; Manchester and Yorkshire about 2¾ hours; and Glasgow about 5½ hours away. Travel between other large towns outside London is also relatively easy. Trains have two classes for passengers: First and Second. Second Class provides good standard upholstered seating but less room compared with First Class. Second Class ticket prices work out very approximately at around £20 per return journey of 200 miles overall. However, for long distances prices per mile tend to be cheaper. As the price of a single journey ticket is rather more than half the cost of a return ticket for the same destination, a traveller who will be returning from his destination should buy a return ticket rather than two single journey tickets. There are concessionary rates for travelling and returning on the same day, and also for travelling at the weekends. If the visitor intends to travel considerably by rail, there are attractively-priced "Rover" tickets valid for seven- or fourteen-day periods. The traveller should enquire carefully at the station ticket office for advice on the cheapest way of accomplishing his journey. ABC Railway Guides are available from bookstalls on station platforms.

There is also a National Bus Service centred on Victoria Station in London. Bus fares are lower than rail fares but the journey times are longer. Internal air flights are also available from Heathrow, but it is generally only really economic to utilise such services for visiting distant regional centres such as Belfast in Northern Ireland or Scotland.

## Car Hire and Traffic

Car hire services are freely available but a driving licence will be required. If the driving licence is not in English, then it would be advisable to obtain an international driving licence before visiting the UK if it is intended to hire a car. Driving is on the left-hand side of the road. When crossing the road near-side traffic will approach from the right.

## Business Centres

London is the most important commercial centre and for most types of goods it should be possible to find a sizeable range of importers with offices situated within that city. However, the import trade is by no means confined to the London area and very many substantial importers often find it advantageous to have offices and warehouses well away from London because of high rents and other costs, and also in order to serve more closely individual regional centres. The exporter should, therefore, be prepared to travel to locations outside London and not seek to confine his business contacts to within a few miles of Central London. Willingness to visit somewhat less accessible importers may prove very worthwhile. Populations of the largest cities in April 1981 were as follows:

| | |
|---|---|
| Greater London | 6,696,000 |
| Birmingham | 1,006,900 |
| Glasgow | 792,200 |
| Leeds | 705,000 |
| Sheffield | 536,800 |
| Liverpool | 510,300 |
| Bradford | 457,700 |
| Manchester | 449,200 |
| Edinburgh | 419,200 |
| Bristol | 388,000 |
| Belfast | 345,800 |
| Coventry | 314,100 |
| Cardiff | 273,900 |

## Weights and Measures

The UK is gradually going over to the metric system of weights and measures. However, the traditional system is still widely employed. Brief conversion tables are as follows:

1 inch = 2.54 centimetres
1 foot = 30.48 centimetres
1 yard = 0.914 metre
1 mile = 1.609 kilometres
1 ounce (oz) = 28.35 grammes
1 pound (lb) = 0.454 kilogramme
1 hundredweight (cwt) = 50.8 kilogrammes
1 ton = 1.016 tonnes
1 pint = 0.568 litre
1 gallon = 4.546 litres

Temperatures may still be given in Fahrenheit:

0° Centigrade = 32° Fahrenheit
20° Centigrade = 68° Fahrenheit
100° Centigrade = 212° Fahrenheit

## Mains Power Supply

Mains power supply in the UK is 415/240 volts 5Hz. Domestic electrical equipment generally operates on 240 volts. This is 20 volts higher than the standard for most European countries, and sensitive equipment such as film projectors set for 220 volts may have to be adjusted.

# UK Imports from Developing Countries (1980)

| SITC section | | £m |
|---|---|---|
| 0 | Food and live animals chiefly for food | 1358.3 |
| 1 | Beverages and tobacco | 133.7 |
| 2 | Inedible crude materials (hides, wood, fibres, ores, etc.) | 799.2 |
| 3 | Mineral fuels, lubricants, etc. | 3992.5 |
| 4 | Animal and vegetable oils, fats and waxes | 107.8 |
| 5 | Chemicals and related products | 79.7 |
| 6 | Manufactured materials (leather, paper, yarn, metals, etc.) | 1124.1 |
| 7 | Machinery and transport equipment | 907.1 |
| 8 | Miscellaneous manufactured articles | 1130.9 |
| 9 | Other transactions | 660.5 |
| | Total | 10,293.8  (20%) |
| | | All imports 51,650.3 |

Source: UK Overseas Trade Statistics

# Some Useful Publications

| *Title*<br>(Comments) | *Where obtainable* |
|---|---|
| *Agency Agreements in the Export Trade*<br>(with specimen agreements) | The Institute of Export<br>(see Useful Addresses) |
| *Directory of British Associations*<br>(Directory of British Trade Associations) | 154 High Street<br>Beckenham<br>Kent<br>England |
| *Croner's Reference Book for Importers*<br>(Details of UK import regulations) | Croner Publications Ltd.<br>Croner House<br>173 Kingston Road<br>New Malden<br>Surrey KT3 3SS |
| *Croner's Reference Book for Exporters*<br>(Details of documentation requirements<br>and export regulations in countries other<br>than the UK) | Croner Publications Ltd.<br>(Address – see above) |
| *HM Customs & Excise Tariff*<br>(Details of import duties, etc.) | HMSO<br>PO Box 569<br>London SE1 |
| *Customs Import Statistics*<br>(Details of British imports by tariff<br>heading) | HM Customs & Excise<br>Portcullis House<br>27 Victoria Avenue<br>Southend-on-Sea<br>Essex |
| *An Introduction to Exporting*<br>(Definitions and illustrations of key<br>documents) | Barclays Bank International Ltd.<br>54 Lombard Street<br>London EC3P 3AH |
| *Elements of Export Practice*<br>(A textbook on exporting) | The Institute of Export<br>(see Useful Addresses) |
| *How to Export Goods* | Croner Publications Ltd.<br>(see above) |
| *Exhibition Bulletin*<br>(Calendar and details of British Fairs<br>and Exhibitions) | 226/272 Kirkdale Road<br>Sydenham<br>London SE26 4RZ |

| *Title*<br>(Comments) | *Where obtainable* |
|---|---|
| *The Grocer*<br>(Leading weekly publication on British retail food trade) | 5 Southwark Street<br>London SE1 |
| International Trade Centre<br>UNCTAD/GATT Publications<br>(Numerous publications on export markets. Major source for export market information) | ITC UNCTAD/GATT<br>Palais des Nations<br>1211 Geneva 10<br>Switzerland |
| *The Directory of British Importers*<br>(Classified list of UK importers) | Trade Research Publications<br>6 Beech Hill Court<br>Berkhamsted<br>Herts HP4 2PR |
| Kompass Directories<br>(Major trade directories published on a country basis) | Kompass Publishers Ltd.<br>Windsor Court<br>East Grinstead<br>West Sussex RH19 1XD |
| Kelly's Directories<br>(Major UK trade directory) | Kelly's Directories<br>Dorset House<br>Stamford Street<br>London SE1 |
| *Legal Aspects of Export Sales*<br>(Textbook on the law governing export sales) | The Institute of Export<br>(see Useful Addresses) |
| *Documentary Letters of Credit*<br>(Definition and illustration of documents concerned with negotiating Letters of Credit) | Barclays Bank International Ltd.<br>54 Lombard Street<br>London EC3P 3AH |
| *Export Marketing Decisions*<br>(Textbook on export marketing) | The Institute of Export<br>(see Useful Addresses) |
| *The Public Ledger*<br>(Details of commodity prices) | Penn House<br>Rickmansworth<br>Herts WB3 1SN |
| *Elements of Shipping*<br>(Textbook on shipping practice) | The Institute of Export<br>(see Useful Addresses) |
| *Dictionary of Shipping & International Trade Terms and Abbreviations* | The Institute of Export<br>(see Useful Addresses) |
| *Tropical Products Institute Publications*<br>(A wide range of publications concerning preparation and marketing of agricultural goods and products) | Tropical Products Institute<br>56/62 Gray's Inn Road<br>London WC1X 13LU |
| *Guide to Incoterms*<br>(Detailed description of internationally recognised standard trade terms) | ICC Services S.a.r.l.<br>Cours Albert 1er<br>75008 Paris<br>France |

# Some Useful Addresses

| Organisation and address | Assistance given |
|---|---|
| Association of British Chambers of Commerce<br>Sovereign House<br>212/224 Shaftesbury Avenue<br>London WC2 | Addresses and information on Chambers of Commerce throughout the United Kingdom. |
| British Agents Register<br>17 Victoria Avenue<br>Harrogate<br>Yorkshire | Addresses of UK agents. |
| British Consultants Bureau<br>1 Westminster Palace Gardens<br>Artillery Row<br>London SW1 | Information on UK business consultancy services. |
| British Export Houses Association (BEHA)<br>69 Cannon Street<br>London EC4N 5AB | Addresses of its export house members. Will circulate trade enquiries to its membership. |
| British Importers Confederation (BIC)<br>69 Cannon Street<br>London EC4N 5AB | Addresses of its members. Will circulate trade enquiries to its membership. |
| British Standards Institution<br>101 Pentonville Road<br>London N1 | Advice and publications on product standards for the UK market. |
| British Tourist Authority<br>Business Travel Department<br>239 Old Marylebone Road<br>London NW1 5QT | Useful information for business visitors to the UK on hotels, etc. |
| Confederation of British Industry (CBI)<br>Centre Point<br>New Oxford Street<br>London WC1 | Principal association of British Industry. May help to provide contacts for developing country enterprises seeking technical co-operation, etc. |
| Her Majesty's Stationery Office (HMSO)<br>PO Box 569<br>London SE1 | Government publications and regulations obtainable by post. |

| Organisation and address | Assistance given |
|---|---|
| International Trade Centre UNCTAD/GATT Palais des Nations 1211 Geneva 10 Switzerland | Leading international agency concerned with trade development. Produces an impressive range of publications on individual markets for a wide range of goods, both primary and manufactured. |
| The Institute of Export World Trade Centre London E1 9AA | Education programmes and examinations in the business of exporting. |
| Institute of Freight Forwarders Suffield House 9 Paradise Road Richmond Surrey TW9 1SA | Addresses of UK freight forwarders. |
| Institute of Linguists 24A Highbury Grove London N5 | Addresses of translation bureaux and interpretation services. |
| Institute of Marketing Moor Hall Cookham Maidenhead Berkshire SL6 9QH | Addresses of marketing organisations and training courses. |
| Intervention Board for Agricultural Produce Fountain House 2 West Mall Butt's Centre Reading RG1 7QW | Source of information on EEC/ ACP import levies and licences. |
| London Chamber of Commerce & Industry (LCCI) 69 Cannon Street London EC4N 5AB | Largest UK Chamber of Commerce. Will circulate trade enquiries to members. Has extensive commercial library useful to overseas businessmen visiting the UK. |
| Manufacturing Agents Association 13A West Street Reigate Surrey | Addresses of UK agents. |
| Ministry of Agriculture, Fisheries and Food Whitehall Place London WC1 | Source of information on food health and import regulations. |
| Research Association for the Paper & Board Printing and Packaging Industries (PIRA) Randalls Road Leatherhead Surrey KT22 7RU | Advice on printing and packaging. |

| *Organisation and address* | *Assistance given* |
|---|---|
| Tropical Products Institute (TPI)<br>56/62 Gray's Inn Road<br>London WC1X BLU | Information on the quality, packing/packaging and marketing of agricultural products. Also produces an extensive range of publications on the marketing of primary products of tropical origin. This is a UK Government organisation. |
| United Kingdom Trade Agency for Developing Countries (UKTA)<br>69 Cannon Street<br>London EC4N 5AB | Government-assisted organisation answering trade enquiries from developing countries. Will receive personal visits from developing country exporters requiring advice and information. |
| World Trade Centre<br>International House<br>London E1 | International association of exporters. |

British Clothing Industry Association
(See leaflet)

Department of Trade & Industry
Victoria St.,
London

Primary Contact. UoP
Advertising Agency

Export Market Development Division
Commonwealth Secretariat

# Glossary of Terms and Definitions

**Air Waybill.** An Air Waybill concerns shipment by air rather than by boat.

**ACP – European Community Convention (Lomé II).** The second Lomé Convention between the European Community and 62 African, Caribbean and Pacific states entered into force on 1st March 1980 and will operate until 28th February 1985. The Convention provides for unlimited duty-free access for almost all industrial products originating in ACP countries and overseas countries and territories of the European Community. Most agricultural products can enter the Community free or at reduced rates of duty; however, they remain subject to the rules of the Community's Common Agricultural Policy. There are special arrangements governing ACP/EEC trade in beef, rum, bananas and sugar.

Requests for further information on Lomé II should be addressed to:
The Commission of the European Communities
Directorate-General (VIII)
Rue de la Loi 200, 1049 Brussels
or its overseas offices.

**Bill of Lading (B/L).** The Bill of Lading (sometimes shortened to Blading) is issued by a shipping company as a receipt for goods accepted for shipment. It is evidence that a contract exists between the exporter and shipping company, and it is also a document of title to the goods concerned. The Bill of Lading will normally give a brief description of the goods, specify the name of the shipper, the carrying vessel, the ports of shipment and discharge, details of any identifying marks on the goods and the name of the person to be notified when the goods arrive. The Bill of Lading will be stamped either "freight paid" or "freight payable at destination" depending on whether the cost of the freight is being paid in advance or not. Depending upon the terms of the export transaction, the importer may require a set of Bills of Lading in order to clear the goods concerned when they reach the discharge (destination) port. In addition to negotiable Bills, non-negotiable copies can also be obtained and these are clearly marked "non-negotiable". Such copies are used for information purposes only, and may be sent to the importer in advance, while the bank will be holding the negotiable Bills against payment by the importer.

**Bills of Exchange.** This is a legal instrument for payment drawn up by the seller (exporter) who is called the "drawer" and sent to the buyer (importer) who is called the "drawee" who has agreed to accept (sign) the Bill. Once the Bill has been accepted by the drawee (importer) it is returned to the drawer (exporter) who can then present it to the drawee at the date stipulated on the Bill for payment. Sometimes the payment date will be designated "sight" which means that the Bill is payable when presented. However, more frequently, the Bill of Exchange is used when the seller wishes to give the buyer (importer) credit. In such a case, the Bill of Exchange is called a "term Bill" to be paid a defined number of days (the due date), usually 30, 60, 90 or 180 days from the acceptance of the Bill by the importer. The Bill can be sent by the exporter to a bank in the importer's country with instructions for the bank to present the Bill when it is due for payment. When appropriate, the exporter can also arrange with the bank that shipping documents enabling the importer to possess the goods concerned will only be handed over by the bank against payment of the Bill. Failure to pay when a Bill of Exchange is presented at its due date of expiry would enable the drawer (exporter) to open legal proceedings against the drawee (importer). Banks will often lend against Bills of Exchange. They may also purchase the Bill of Exchange at a discount related to the rate of interest and the risk involved by asking the drawer to endorse the Bill over to themselves. This means the bank takes over the rights of the drawer against the drawee.

**Bank – Opening.** An Opening Bank is one which opens the Letter of Credit on the importer's instructions.

**Bank – Correspondent.** A correspondent bank is a bank in the exporter's country related to the opening bank in the importer's country. It may merely pass on information from the opening bank (when it is designated the advising bank) or it may be given authority in the L/C established by the opening bank to "negotiate" the exporter's documents against payment. This means the exporter does not have to send his shipping documents abroad in order to receive payment.

**Conference/Liner Shipping Services.** On most of the frequented trade routes, shipping companies, individually or collectively, provide scheduled regular shipping services. This means that the exporter can plan his exports for specific sailing dates. When conference/liner shipping services are not available, the exporter may nevertheless be able to find a suitable vessel calling at his port to receive his goods, depending upon the utilisation of the port concerned. However, he may not be able to advise the importer in advance on sailing dates, and it may be difficult to undertake regular shipments.

**Charter Shipping.** In the case of bulk cargoes, the exporter may find it necessary to charter his own vessel to export his goods. Chartering a vessel could involve the exporter in unexpected costs due to port delays, but for some bulk commodities this method of shipment may be the only way of being competitive. There are specialist companies acting as chartering agents. As chartering can involve risk and complications, the inexperienced exporter should hope to sell on an FOB basis and leave chartering to an experienced importer.

**Delivery, Discharge or Destination Point.** The delivery, discharge or destination point is the location applying to the agreed Trade Term. This location should always be added, e.g. FOB Lagos, CIF London, or DDP Coventry.

**Exchange Control.** A system of governmental control on the acquisition and use of foreign exchange or currency.

**The EEC.** The European Economic Community is an economic grouping of countries which currently consists of Belgium, Denmark, France, West Germany, Greece, Holland, Italy, Luxemburg, Ireland and the UK, and negotiates trade matters jointly. (See ACP — European Community Convention (Lomé II) and Generalised Scheme of Preferences.)

**Forwarding Agents.** A forwarding agent is a specialised enterprise which is employed by the exporter to advise on shipment and organise activities involved in the shipment of his goods. The term "freight agent", and "receiving agent" are by-and-large equivalent. The forwarding agent will normally play a key role in export shipments unless the exporter is able to handle all the shipping documentation himself, and is prepared to work out freight costs and negotiate with shipping companies. Normally, only large firms which are big enough to employ a staff of shipping specialists will be able to do without the services of a forwarding agent.

**Forwarding Agent's Receipt.** A forwarding agent's receipt is a document issued by a forwarding agent confirming that the goods concerned are now held to his "order", meaning he has taken them under his control. Such a document may frequently be utilised instead of a Bill of Lading, especially in the case of overland shipments. It is not, however, a document of title; but is acceptable evidence that the exporter has commenced shipment, and in the appropriate circumstances may be designated as one of the negotiating documents required under a Letter of Credit.

**Forwarding Agent's Through Bill.** A forwarding agent's Through Bill is a document issued by a forwarding agent stating that the goods are being shipped to a specified destination. As in the case of forwarding agent's receipt it is not a document of title, but is sometimes used instead of a Bill of Lading, especially when shipments may involve utilising different modes of transport, or several trans-shipments where a normal Bill of Lading is not obtainable.

**Goods.** Throughout the publication the general term "goods" has been employed to denote all forms of merchandise from raw materials and commodities to manufactured and industrial products. Although the range of goods which may be exported is vast, all export transactions have at least some features in common.

**Generalised Scheme of Preferences (GSP).** Most developed countries operate a GSP, which offers preferential tariff treatment to exports from developing countries with the aim of increasing the developing countries' export earnings, encouraging their industrialisation, and speeding up their economic growth. The European Community's GSP, first introduced in 1971 and which the United Kingdom joined in 1974, was substantially revised in 1980 and extended for a further ten years in 1981.

Almost all industrial products are granted duty-free access, though a number of products of particular sensitivity to the Community industry may be subject to quantitative limits, but these do not apply to.the Least Developed Countries. Preferential access is also given to a range of agricultural products, usually without quantitative limits but often at reduced rather than zero rates of duty. The Least Developed Countries enjoy some special concession for these agricultural products. Preferences for textile products covered by the Multi-Fibre Arrangements (MFA) are reserved for products originating in those developing countries which have bilateral arrangements with the Community within the framework of the MFA. However, there are special arrangements for textile exports from the Least Developed Countries.

In order to qualify for benefit under the GSP, imported goods have to conform to origin and consignment rules. To qualify as "originating" the goods must have been wholly produced (e.g. grown, mined) in the beneficiary country or, if they were made from any materials not wholly produced there, they must have complied with certain rules concerning the use of imported materials in their manufacture. Generally, a consignment of goods is admissable under the GSP only if it was consigned and transported direct from the beneficiary country to the Community.

The European Community revises its scheme each year and the details are published in the Official Journal of the European Communities. Copies of this and any further information can be obtained from:
The Commission of the European Communities
Directorate-General for External Relations
Rue de la Loi 200, 1040 Brussels
or its overseas offices.

**Invoice (Commercial).** The Invoice is a key document which is utilised in most transactions. It is issued by the seller and will specify the goods sold, their quantity, their price to the buyer, and the terms of payment. An Invoice will be normally required for payment, and in some transactions will be the only document against which payment is made. For instance, an Invoice might be the sole payment document presented to the buyer in a DDP contract. Payment against Invoice alone will tend to be utilised by exporters (sellers) who have complete confidence in the importer's (buyer's) willingness and ability to pay.

**Invoice (Pro Forma).** The Pro Forma Invoice is similar, as far as the details it contains, to the commercial or ordinary invoice. However, by being headed with the words "Pro Forma" it ceases to be a demand for payment. An importer may request the exporter to issue him with a Pro Forma Invoice as a means of confirmation of the main terms of the contract sale, and also to assist him in opening an L/C through his bank. The commercial invoice will be sent later, around the time the goods are shipped.

**Invoice (Certified).** A Certified Invoice is one which has been stamped or sealed by a Chamber of Commerce, Commercial or Consular Office, or other authorised authority. Certified Invoices are not normally required when exporting to the UK, but may be required in the case of many other countries. Of course, goods from origins entitled to preferential duty treatment should be accompanied by GSP Form A or EUR 1 in the case of ACP/Lomé countries. These forms certify the origin of the goods concerned.

**Insurance Certificate.** An Insurance Certificate is a document obtainable from an insurance company in which the insurance company agrees to indemnify the assured against loss or damage to the goods insured. The insurance company charges the assured (insured) a premium for this service.

**Levy System (EEC).** Some agricultural products from developing countries exported to EEC countries such as the UK will be subject to the EEC Levy System. The Levy is a special kind of import duty which has the objective of raising the price of imported agricultural goods to the price level ruling within the EEC. Because of this, the Levy rate tends to vary depending upon the difference between average world market prices and prices for the agricultural products concerned within the EEC. Some developing countries who are traditional suppliers of agricultural products to the EEC, while remaining subject to the Levy, receive preferential treatment under the Levy System.

**Least Developed Countries.** Certain of the poorest developed countries who are not members of the ACP/Lomé group receive especially favourable treatment under the GSP System.

**Letter of Credit (L/C).** Letters of Credit are also called documentary credits. A Letter of Credit (L/C) is an instrument by which the importer assures payment to the exporter. The importer requests his bank to open a Letter of Credit made payable to the named exporter against the receipt of specified documents such as a Bill of Lading, insurance certificate, invoice, etc. The L/C can be either revocable or irrevocable, but nowadays revocable L/Cs are seldom opened. This means that once the L/C is opened by the bank, the importer cannot ask the bank to withdraw it. An L/C can also be "confirmed". The exporter receiving payment under an L/C in his own country through a Correspondent Bank (see note) may request the importer to ask the Opening Bank (see note) to have the payment confirmed by the Correspondent Bank. This will result in an extra charge, but the exporter has the advantage of having his payment guaranteed, assuming the documents are correct, by a bank in his own country without recourse to the Opening Bank in the importer's country. Once the exporter has received an L/C from the importer, he can usually use this document as a means of security with his own bank if he needs to borrow to finance the export. Every Letter of Credit will have an expiry date after which it is no longer negotiable. The exporter will be dependent upon the importer's goodwill for extending the date of the Letter of Credit if he cannot present his documents before its expiry date.

**The Multi-Fibre Arrangement (MFA).** The MFA regulates international trade in textiles and clothing and has recently been extended to operate until July 1986. Products covered by the MFA are divided into carefully-defined categories which are subject to quotas for each country exporting to the European Community under an MFA Agreement. The system operates by the importing country issuing import licences up to the quota level only against valid export certificates issued by the exporting country. The MFA provides for the introduction of new quotas if trade volumes reach specified levels and for some growth in the size of quotas from year to year.

Detailed information on how the MFA works and what action exporters should take if they wish to export textiles to the UK is obtainable from:
International Trade Policy Division, Branch 3
Department of Trade
1–19 Victoria Street
London SW1    Tel. 01-215 5350.

**Mail Payment.** Mail Payment means that the payment instructions from one bank to another are sent by airmail rather than by cable or telex. The speed of payment will therefore depend upon the speed of the postal services involved.

**Nominated Vessel.** A Nominated Vessel is one designated by the importer on which he wishes his goods to be shipped.

**Open General Licence.** This means that goods can be imported without need to apply for any specific import licence.

**Packing List.** A Packing List is one of the shipping documents normally required by the importer. A packing list itemises the individual pieces of cargo, e.g. sacks, bales, cartons, drums, etc., and designates the weight or dimensions of each piece and their contents. Each piece on the packing list may be identified by Shipping Marks.

**Stale Bills.** Bills of Lading which reach the importer's possession after arrival of the vessel concerned at the destination port are called "stale" Bills of Lading. Depending upon the contract terms Stale Bills may enable the importer to repudiate the contract, or claim for damages.

**Shipping Company.** A Shipping Company is an enterprise controlling means of transport such as ships. It makes a "freight charge" for its carrying services. A shipping company can issue Bills of Lading.

**Shipping Agent.** A Shipping Agent is an enterprise acting for a shipping company or companies. It can receive instructions and negotiate on behalf of a shipping company. Shipping agents frequently combine the functions of forwarding agents.

**Shipping Marks.** Shipping Marks is the name given to some clear means of identification which the importer may require the exporter to place on each individual sack, bale, carton, etc. This will enable the goods to be easily identified when they arrive in the importer's country.

**Shipment Date.** The Shipment Date is the date at which shipment is to be effected. Shipment dates are usually approximate and are normally stated as part of the contracted shipment terms, e.g. FOB Lagos end December, or CIF London mid-September. These examples mean that the goods have to be delivered to Lagos in time for shipment on board the vessel at the end of December, or in the case of the CIF London contract that the goods should arrive in London by mid-September.

**Shut Out.** Sometimes goods that have been "booked" on a vessel are "shut out", that is not "received" for shipment; either due to their late arrival on the quayside, or because the vessel has been "over-booked" and is unable to receive any more cargo. In view of this, it is better for goods to arrive early for shipment on the vessel concerned rather than at the last moment.

**Trans-shipment.** When shipment to a certain destination cannot be accomplished on one vessel alone due to a lack of a vessel sailing directly between the two ports concerned, the goods will have to be transferred from one vessel to another at an intervening port or possibly ports. Importers are sometimes reluctant to accept trans-shipment because of the increased likelihood of loss or damage to the goods when they are trans-shipped. It is possible to obtain Bills of Lading (called Through Bills) even when several different vessels are involved in transporting the cargo to its destination port. These Bills will be issued by a shipping company and, unlike the forwarding agent's Through Bill, are documents of title.

**Telegraphic Transfer (TT).** The Telegraphic Transfer is the quickest means of transferring payment funds from one country to another. This is accomplished by the bank in the paying country telexing or cabling a bank in the receiving country where the importer resides to make a prompt payment to his account. The receiving bank debits the account of the paying bank.

**Tariffs.** A Tariff is another term for import duty.

## Trade Terms/Shipping Terms

**FOB (Free on Board).** The term FOB means the exporter is responsible for delivering the goods to be placed on a vessel or aircraft at the designated port or airport. All costs until the goods are placed on board the vessel or aircraft concerned are payable by the exporter.

**C&F (Cost and Freight).** The term C&F means the exporter is responsible for shipping the goods to the importer's discharge port and all costs of such shipment, excluding insurance, are borne by the exporter. As a result of the containerisation of many cargoes, C&F and CIF terms are often extended to an Inland Customs Clearance Depot beyond the port of entry. When the containers are discharged from the vessel they can be transported sealed to an inland depot for Customs clearance. Such a depot may be nearer to the importer's warehouse than the port.

**CIF (Cost/Insurance/Freight).** The term CIF is the same as C&F except that the exporter is also responsible for insuring the goods during shipment on behalf of the importer.

**Freight and Carriage Paid.** This term means the exporter is responsible for all freight including inland carriage costs to a destination within the importer's country agreed in the contract. This destination is usually the importer's warehouse. Normally, the importer is responsible for the insurance, unless stipulated otherwise, as well as any import duties, etc.

**DDP (Delivered Duty Paid).** The term DDP means the exporter is responsible for delivering the goods from his country all the way to the buyer's (importer's) warehouse or premises. As well as being responsible for shipment, the exporter will also be responsible for clearing the goods through the discharge port and Customs and paying any import duties. Unless the exporter has an office in the importer's country he is likely to employ the services of a forwarding agent in the importing country to undertake these activities. Because of the need to have foreign exchange to pay inland freight costs and import duties, if chargeable, DDP contracts may not be possible for exporters from many developing countries.

## Incoterms

Standard conditions and rules governing trade terms have been established by the International Chamber of Commerce. These standard terms are called "Incoterms". For a full description of the obligations of the exporter and importer under each "Incoterm", the exporter is referred to the *Guide to Incoterms* published by ICC Services S.a.r.l., 38 Cours Albert 1er, 75008 Paris, France. The exporter can use this publication to obtain a comprehensive understanding of Trade Terms.

APPENDIX F

# Tariff Preference Quotas

Nearly all developing countries are able to export to the UK on a preferential duty basis under the GSP system, that is their goods pay less than the standard rate of duty when imported into the UK. For most products originating from ACP and Least Developed Countries, there will be no duty payable at all. (See notes on ACP and GSP in the Glossary.) However, for trade "sensitive" items, this preferential duty treatment is limited by quota. That means that when the UK preferential import duty quota for the article concerned is exhausted, the full rate of duty or levy (for some agricultural goods) is payable. Quota limits for each country are administered separately, except for certain handmade products from 21 specified countries when the quota is treated globally. Full details of the tariff quota system are given in Part 11 of HM Customs & Excise Tariff. Information, particularly concerning exhausted quotas, may be obtained from:

Central Tariff Quota Unit,
International Customs Division D, Branch 6,
King's Beam House,
Mark Lane,
London EC3R 7HE.

To benefit from the preferential rate whether subject to quota or not, an appropriate certificate of origin (usually GSP Form A or EUR 1) must be supplied. Eligibility for the preferential duty treatment under the quota system operates under the "first come, first served" basis, that is the quota is filled up in date order of entry of the goods through HM Customs. There is an exception for certain frozen-meat quotas. Depending on how quickly the quota is likely to be exhausted, it is advisable to export near the commencement date of the quota rather than later. For some types of goods, the quota may be exhausted in a few days, for others it is usually never exhausted.

Textiles imported by MFA Group Countries (see note on MFA) may receive preferential duty treatment. However, textile goods from countries in the Multi-Fibre Arrangement are subject to import licensing quotas which means no more goods can be imported after the quota is filled, and the option of paying the full rate of duty is not available.

If goods arrive in the UK after the tariff preference quota is exhausted, the importer can store the goods in a Customs warehouse where duty payment is suspended as long as the goods remain in the warehouse. The importer must calculate the cost and inconvenience of storing the goods until a new tariff preference quota comes into force (usually the beginning of the year), against any extra duty which will have to be paid if the goods are imported at the non-quota rate.

In the case of quotas for handloom fabrics, eligible goods must be exclusively woven by hand or foot, must have a prescribed certificate of manufacture from a

70

recognised authority in the country of origin; each piece of fabric must carry an approved stamp at each end, or a single approved lead seal, and they must be transported directly from the country of manufacture to the European Community/UK.

Least Developed Countries are likely to receive exceptionally favourable import tariff treatment and for the most part are not likely to be subject to tariff or licensing quotas. At present, these countries are: Afghanistan, Bangladesh, Botswana, Cape Verde, Ethiopia, Guinea, Guinea Bissau, Haiti, Lesotho, Malawi, Maldives, Nepal, São Tomé and Principe, Sudan, Tanzania, Tonga, Upper Volta, Western Samoa, Yemen North, Yemen South.

# New Exporter's Code

1. Always answer telexes and letters promptly.
2. Always investigate the requirements of the market concerned with the utmost seriousness.
3. Always supply goods as per sample or agreed specification.
4. Always ship goods by the time agreed.
5. Always pay close attention to the terms of the business contract.
6. Always keep business appointments.
7. Always plan ahead.

# Index